Trajectories to the Moon

Sarah McBride

chipmunkapublishing

the mental health publisher

Trajectories to the Moon

All rights reserved, no part of this publication may be reproduced by any means, electronic, mechanical photocopying, documentary, film or in any other format without prior written permission of the publisher.

Published by

Chipmunkapublishing

PO Box 6872

Brentwood

Essex CM13 1ZT

United Kingdom

http://www.chipmunkapublishing.com

Copyright © Sarah McBride 2010

Chipmunkapublishing gratefully acknowledge the support of Arts Council England.

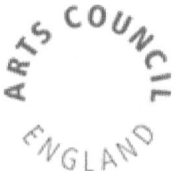

Author Biography

Born to Jack and Annie McBride, on the first of March 1938, in a beautiful County Antrim glen called Glenariff, Sarah already had an older brother, named John,

11 months later a girl Kathleen was born to Annie, soon after she developed post natal depression, and was admitted to the psychiatric hospital, in the town of Antrim.

Sarah, John and Kathleen went to live with their grand mother and father, at Garren Point, County Antrim. Mrs Sarah O'Kane was the post mistress her husband John O'Kane was a coast guard.

So began a happy 4 years at Garren Point, with a post office home shared by 4 aunties who were very kind. Sarah's grandmother was strict but fair. Sarah remembers skipping from rock to rock beside the Atlantic Ocean which her grandmother's house backed on to. There was a shingle shore where flotsam and jetsam provided a source of many happy hours of play for the three children.

It was during one of these play sessions when Sarah was five, that her auntie Kathleen came to tell the three children that their mother had come to see them. Sarah remembers seeing a fat lady in a navy blue suit with her arm resting on the post office counter.

Within two weeks Sarah and her brother and sister were bundled off to Glenariff, the good part of this being her father was there. Sarah was very close to her father. He had continued to visit his children at the post office, during his wife's illness. Taking them for picnics on Sundays and recounting many fairy stories to them. Jack Mcbride was a reporter on the Ballymena Observer and was also a journalist. His articles being published in local newspapers he also had a radio program called 'The Bard' which ran for 7 years on BBC1 N.I., in later years he published a book called 'Traveller in the Glen'.

Sarah McBride continued to live in Glenariff where she attended Gilmore primary school where she excelled in English.

Later passing the 11 plus examination and winning a scholarship to St. Louis High School in Ballymena where she continued to excel at English and was good at music too. However she did not fit in at school and left at just 15. Sarah then took a job in a shop at Cushindun and from there went to work in a residential home for children at Larne.

When Sarah was 18 she joined the RAF and came to England, spending a happy 18 months, in the service.

Returning to Northern Ireland she was employed by the blood transfusion service a job she held for 3 years.

Sarah then trained and worked as a nurse doing stints at General, Psychiatric and Mentally Handicap hospitals.

Sarah was a student nurse in a psychiatric hospital in Gloucester when she became pregnant with her oldest son Jonathan. The father was not in a position to marry her though he would have liked too.

So she found herself in a mother and baby home in Bristol where Jonathan was born at South Meads hospital.

Sarah then took a live in nursing job at Bridgwater Somerset where she met Brian Cavill, the man who was to become her husband. They married in Jan 1967. Sarah had a happy 6 months when in June 1967 Jonathan contracted T.B. Meningitis he was in a coma for 6 weeks and was badly brain damaged.

Sarah and Brian took him home and looked after him as best they could, while Jonathan was in a coma his sister Angela was born.

After Sarah's fourth and last child was born she was diagnosed bi-polar disorder and spent many months over the following years in Psychiatric units. The result was her marriage broke down and was divorced in 2005

Sarah was separated when she met William Dodd (Billy) they have an instant rapport and in 2008 he asked her to move in with him. This she did and is very happy, hoping to be married to him next year, 2010.

Trajectories to the Moon

The Book

Sarah uses her many life experiences to explore the human psyche. Sarah's love of words and the poignant pictures they evoke shine through in many of her pieces of work. Although many of the subjects are of a serious nature her profound sense of humour and her understanding of the absurdity of life are self evident.

This book will appeal to a wide audience, each picking out a particular poem that communicates to them as an individual. Sarah's use of words to paint mind pictures, such as two little shoes, where she uses that as a symbolism of loss, will catch the imagination that perhaps visual art some times can not.

Trajectories to the Moon

Sarah McBride

"Trajectories" to the moon

I am a mental illness
And I come in many guises
I have many interchangeable names
(Bipolar Affective Disorder
Now takes the place of manic depression)
Which name reigned supreme
For many decades
I have many facets
And I can disrupt people's lives.
Oh how I love to do that!
As soon as I see a chink
In anyone's armour - I am in
The chink in armour can be
Protein builds up in the brain
Causing Alzheimer's
Or chemical imbalance due to drugs
Be they legal or illegal
Once I am in I take great delight
In changing a person's personality for the worse
What once would have been anathema
To those I affect – this is what
I can make them do
Become so obsessive about cleanliness
That they wash over and over again
Leaving no time for normal living
How I rub my hands in glee
When I see my powers at work
And how I laugh at the caricatures
Of themselves people have become
I am called mental illness
A euphemism under which umbrella
I can wreak havoc undeterred
I can rob folk of their motivation
Making others see them as lazy

Trajectories to the Moon

And keeping a constant eye on this
I see to it – it is called M.E.
I get enjoyment from that name
Which seems so innocuous
Nobody thinks it is me
I can make life so intolerable for folk
Many take their own lives
A pity that – I can no longer torment them
But when I see grieving relatives
My cup is full – because of the trauma
If only three or four succumb to me
A mental illness – it will all have been worthwhile
I can make people go off at tangents
Thinking they can send "trajectories"
To the moon by the power of thought
Read other people's thoughts – or that
Everyone is reading theirs
I should be congratulated on this
Un sure all would agree
It's a particularly clever trick of mine
I can make people hear voices
Which they find very hard to deal with
So real to them they – having battled
Against me for so long – are overtaken
And sometimes not always they become so violent they have to be restrained
I have such a fancy name for this
Some people cannot even spell me
I am Schizophrenia and I take away
Peoples dignity so that they'll run
Out of doors naked if told to by my voices
Young people are so affected sometimes
To the point that they break a window
This causes a great uproar and disturbance
And I am delighted to say many people may spend
A night in a prison cell
I also cause intrusive thoughts which have

Sarah McBride

A bearing (pardon the pun) on behaviour too
Similar to voices my intrusive thoughts
Can send some people manic
Dancing – singing – out of control
I can manipulate people's minds
So that they become disinhibited
I think it's a sexual disinhibition
That I am most fond of
I can cause fornication, bestiality
And sodomy – all under the disguise
Of myself – a mental illness
I see to it that folk affected
Rationalise it away beautifully
In fact, most of the people forget
What they've done while under my influence
The few who do remember are
A thorn in the side to me
They could give the game away completely
If I'm not careful
Which brings me on the Psychological games
Oh! How I like to play Psychological games!
My friends are ignorance, pride
Gullibility and arrogance
My enemy those who have insight
And see me for what I really am.

Trajectories to the Moon

Inexact Sciences and Terminological Inexactitudes of the Gods

From out of the mists of medication
I have come – to a crystal mind –
Thirty – one years lost.
Bitter – angry – recriminatory?
I am all of these and none
Can I now, in retrospect, describe
The horror, hurt – the degradation?
Thoughts mill – the past that has
Shaped my present self
The immediacy is that I must
Write – tell – for I remember well
Diagnosis – stabs in the back-
Character stolen - lost
Schizophrenia – Manic Depression
Now Bi – polar affective disorder
Paranoia, obsessive compulsive disorder
Spurious gobbledegook about vulnerable
People – spawned to perpetuate
The myth of the superior mind of the god
So these gods can be surrounded
By mystique – who can call us to account?

Labels – notes – opinions given
From so many different sources
How can a picture true emerge?

Mind altering drugs – legal
Don't forget they're LEGAL
Mind altering drugs
Astoundingly – abominably still given
For now its known – so that
It is inexcusable
Pronouncements still made – the
Gobbledegook and 'medication' still

Sarah McBride

Rammed down each psychiatric patients
Throat or 'up their bum'
Patients bow to the greater wisdom
Of their would be masters.

It will not end without a fight
From within – it will not end
While the pharmaceutical giants
Grab – and there are large amounts
Of money in the making. Surely
These people could deploy their
Expertise to better end?

Let the biochemists spend six months within
The constraints of their own chemical concoctions
Let's experiment on them
Soon there'd be some alteration
To the – chop some hexagons off here and add some there
Let the biochemists swallow their own poison
Let's experiment on themWhat fun we have creating our own creations
Hit and miss
Of course we do not call them by such mundane name
No each creation must have an unpronounceable misnomer
Seroxat Mirtazipine Flueroperazinel
We have a predilection for an X or Z
We'd have Xylophone but that's been played
What great names for ourselves we've made

I have come to know people as people
Of whatever religion, class race or psychiatric disposition
No one has the right to look down their nose
At another human being or benefit from their calamity
But those who set themselves up as gods
Lend themselves to a shooting down an equalization
We who have our poems published in James Fergusons book
Will endeavour to do just that

Trajectories to the Moon

By that peaceful of most peaceful weaponry the written word
Do I hear howls of Derision Delusions of Grandeur
From the dissenting gods
If this be the case I will cope as I have always done
Ye gods

Two little shoes

Two little shoes are missing
From the row of shoes by the wall
All polished and ready for school the next day
My heart breaks when I recall

Two little shows are missing
And Ill never get used to that sight
Of three little pairs of shoes by the wall
Where four always sat through the night

Two little shoes are missing
Meningitis took its toll on us all
Two missing shoes where yours should ne
My Jonathan – your name I still call

And the two little shoes that were missing
Wait somewhere else by a wall

Trajectories to the Moon

Winter

Oh to see winter as they used to be
Snow icicles and frost at this special time of year
Now all we have is rain, rain and more rain
(No wonder so many people emigrate to Spain)
I remember winter as it was in childhood
When I attended a little primary school
In the Glens of Antrim- Glenariff-
Where I was born – called the Queen of the
Nine glens because of its exceptional beauty
But there was a bitter side to the winter there
Some children had no shoes and their
Clothes of such poor quality did not keep them warm
We didn't point and say "look at her or him
They've got no shoes on"- life indeed was grim
For all the small farmers all around
They didn't have money- only when they sold
A pig or a cow and that to pay the bills
We had boots and shoes- but we just accepted
That some others didn't and you couldn't help
It would have been charity which would
Have been anathema to them
Yes winter had two faces in those days
Cruel and cold comes to mind
Oh winter where have you gone?
The seasons
Have merged and you no longer have your time
Oh for a good flurry of snow to let us know
You're still around in whatever guise
Come back winter- all is forgiven

Sarah McBride

Star Taxis

Taxi! Star Taxi! Driver's at everyone's beck and call
You need a lot of patience for the folk who may appal
By their use of such expletives-
That even you would not recall
Saturday nights you see some sights
When the pubs are emptied
Both of beer and folk
Who need transporting home
Being incapable to walk

Then there's folk you take to hospitals
Both psychiatric and A and E
You then become as counsellors
Helping people see
That what ever has befallen them
It's not such a tragedy
You driver's really are a special breed
You're there as soon as people need
Transporting from A to B
You have to know the "Knowledge"
Of the counties, towns and road
As a complex as in London
In its own way – quite a load

People expect such a lot from you
You have to gauge each face
Some will be quite chatty
Dare I say it – some quite batty

Then there's folk who speak just gibberish
Making drivers feel quite liverish
If a driver doesn't know at least six languages
(A rarity – though the law of averages says some will)
By gestures and imagination taxi drivers
Can then solve – the destination asked for

Trajectories to the Moon

It's really quite involved
Yes – Star Taxis are the best
In a class above the rest
It's the taxi I used mostly
Where I'm treated as a guest

Sarah McBride

She's bad not mad

The Samaritans I thought were kind trustworthy people
There are some who want to do the job they volunteered to do
But some who don't quite see things very clearly
I was called every day at their behest mind you.
Just phone is back they said – we'll always talk to you
Then THE discussion must have taken place
Sarah is addicted to phoning us one said
A pseudo-director was chosen to deliver
Ludicrous, mind boggling news instead
Sarah must be restricted to phoning once a day
In fact it would be better if she didn't call per se
These grudges that she has against the medical profession
Would be better left unuttered, were not a prod in the
conscience session
We know we told her she could talk to us about just anything
But there's anything and anything and anyway she's mad
Can't have her speaking as she does and making is eel bad
Horror against horror – she writes some poetry too
Indeed - the very thought of it - how stupid can you get
Were above that sort of thing – we never does a winter yet.

Ode to a cup of tea

We asked for a cup of tea this morn
We cannot have it until dawn
At the decree of someone called Staff Nurse
Does he really hold the N.H.S purse
It seems at a whim it was denied
Our request for tea being nullifies
By someone out there with a heart of stone
In thinking this I am not alone
Just put yourself in the patient's place
The long three hours that we have to face
Before a beverage can cross our lips
If this goes on we'll all be on drips
You are part of a very tight-knit clique
Of carers who do not seem to care at all
For the thoughts and feelings that we do recall
You have to stamp your mark on us all
Whether it's a reasonable request you turn down
For doing such things you all have renown
A bigger man had he been at large
Would have granted us our simple plea
And bought us a nice hot cup of tea

Sarah McBride

Notes from a Psychiatric unit

I'm having my head read today
In a contraption that's called an x-ray
It's long overdue
I'm one of the few
Who's escaped through the net
Still – I pray
In slices (oh really?)
I'll be
So the doctors more easily see
What up with my brain
Someone's laughed like a drain
They've seen through my true masquerade

Neighbours

Come rally round all ye neighbours
And flock to my sons review
I know you don't know much of Jonathon
But we really are counting on you
We've exhausted all other potential
With you we will have to make- do
We'll hire a bus and we'll make a big fuss
Do you fancy a day at the Zoo
No offence meant to my sons
Dear friends who have no-one to speak up to them
We'll follow a trend to declare war on the fen
And Jonathon can head to platoon

Judgement

Caught in a clever trap am I
I see it as it meets the eye
You seem to be part of it
I can not see the sense of fit
Around the living day light hours
The lies that seem to come so glib
From off the lips of those who sit
In judgement on the parapet

Brian the Social Worker

Collar turned up and always busy
Us Brian the social worker
Collar turned up what call has he
For the niceties of life
Ever busy seeing to his clients
To my mind he is a kindly
Not for him the brusqueness
Of many in the same profession
He has stored my fail
In human terms and also
From a clients point of view
He has told me he doesn't give a damn
I think he means about the petty
Things in life
As I said before – collar in disarray
What call has he for petty nicety
Where he can help he does not hinder
There's no one I have med who would be kinder.

Sarah McBride

The passing storm (Down the Glen)

Lowering clouds – the advancing storm – the dark gloom of a windswept landscape – these bring back memories for one of my father first and foremost and one of my mother too.

I can see my father now at the front of our cottage down the Glen – Glenariff in the Glens of Antrim, Glenariff named the Queen of the Nine Glens for its exceptional beauty. It will not be long before sheet and folk lightening can be seen illuminating the valley. Where does my father come into all this? There he is at the front door encouraging us, his children, to come and view the spectacle – and my mother – she is in the kitchen so afraid and calling out "Come in you'll all be killed!"

How did this affect us in later life? I cannot speak of my brothers and sisters (there are eleven of us) but for me thunder and lightening has an ambiguity about it. It fascinates and repels me at the same time. Not exactly what my father had in mind when he tried so hard to make it fun for us.
My father was a dreamer and as such was a very good writer indeed – his articles always finding space in local newspapers where he sometimes wrote about the elements through his writing and broadcasting was mostly folklore.

My mother on the other hand balanced the dreamer in my father by being so practical and down to earth hence her feelings that surely we would at least be struck by lightening or at best we were putting ourselves in line for that eventuality.

I never see an electric storm without visualising that particular evening down the Glen when mu dear friend showed – in his own way – how much he loved us. He was trying to prepare us for life – albeit life in the Glens of Antrim 0 where the storms were indeed quite frightening. He could not know at the time that his four children would eventually become scattered to the four corners of the globe. Whenever an electrical storm is encountered do they, like me think of their humble beginnings and the storms that lit up our childhood loves in the valley of our Antrim Glens?

Thunder and lightening will forever be associated with my father and mother because of this evening which is forever etched on my memory.

Sarah McBride

Wonders Will Never Cease (A Play)

Mrs Creepit: Is that social Services?
Secretary: Yes, How can I help?
Mrs C: I'd like to speak to someone involved in my son Tom's case a social worker perhaps
Sec: I'm afraid she's not available
Mrs C: Could you tell me when she would be available?
Sec: No, I could not
Mrs C: Could I perhaps speak to the manager?
Sec: Oh, you mean Fred.
Mrs C: Yes, if I may
Sec: Oh, I'm sorry …. You're out luck.
Fred's in the South of France for a week.
Mrs C: You told me he was in the
Bahamas a fortnight ago- South of France, so soon!
Sec: Is there anything else?
Mrs C: I really do need to speak to someone
Sec: Well just give me your number and I'll get someone to phone you back.
Mrs C: My number is 249621
Sec: I've got that- 294126
Mrs C: I've made a note of it Goodbye, Four days later
Mrs C: Is that social Services
Sec: Yes how can I help?
Mrs C: I phoned four days ago and you told me someone would ring me back
Sec: No-one was available
Mrs C: I'd like to speak to the social worker involved in my sons case
Sec: Oh, you mean Tania
Mrs C: Yes
Sec: She's not available
Mrs C: Could I speak to the manager?
Sec: I'm afraid Fred's no longer with us
Mrs C: Good Lord – when did he die? I offer my sincere condolences

Trajectories to the Moon

Sec: Oh no! He's just popped out to the shop
Mrs C: Could you say when he'll be back
Sec: No I could not
Mrs C: Could I speak to someone else?
Sec: There's nobody here
Mrs C: There's a person I sometimes speak to when nobody's there.
Could I speak to her?
Sec: No you can speak to me
Mrs C: I do feel very let down
Sec: You're not the only one, there's more people like you
Mrs C: I'll phone you again later when maybe someone will be available
Sec: That's what were here for to speak to people and be of help
Mrs C: Thanks for your help- speak to you soon
Sec: Goodbye

Two Hours Later
Mrs C: Is that Social Services?
Sec: Yes, How can I help?
Mrs C: I phoned this morning – is anyone available now?
Sec: Is that Mrs Creepit about Tom?
Mrs C: Yes, I'd like to speak to someone involved with my son Tom
Sec: No-one is available at this time
Mrs C: Could you say when someone would be available?
Sec: Not at the moment
Mrs C: Just rang to say I've got some very good news and the first people I thought of were you, I've just won the lottery
Sec: What's your name again?
Mrs C: Mrs Creepit, you know and Tom
Sec: Well Mrs Creepit, we were just saying the other day what a lovely woman you are – and that son of yours, Tom what potential for someone with Behaviour problems. What Behaviour Problems- we've got your number and we'll be

phoning you back immediately if not sooner, the lottery you
say well wonders never cease

Procrastinators

People who seem to have no sense of time
Shortly means about a two hour wait
Heaven forbid you're told immediately
Never would be a more appropriate time to say
I am from a more precise era when
Length of time people had to wait
"Lies" is perhaps too strong a word
Procrastinators would better fit the bill
The opposite of power is powerless
Ordinary folk do not seem warrant
A prompt response from powers that be
More power to my elbow and my pen
I have written these words immediately
Shortly I might publish them
Don't bother to return my call
I think my poem says it all

Housework

I am galloping after the dusk and grime
Like a man with a polo stick
Each particle which lands in a handy dustpan
Is victory enough for my lick
Not my forte cleaning – though clean I like to be
Its frustrating to see the dust disperse
And settle right down next to me
It really is a laborious job
This housework which has to be done
The best of ones ability
Is never enough for some
Clean, clean, shine, shine
I cannot hear the clock chime
I'm so engrossed in this cleaning grit
Time takes on its own remit
Next time you see a house wife struggle
To keep all a-polish and shine
Give thought to the aforesaid galloping horse
And be 'lighten her yoke' your incline
I know- I'm a galloping horse myself
With all my polish and shine on one shelf
Where it says – mores' the pity- for days on end
While I think about writing a poem to suit
Or maybe sell at the next car boot

Trajectories to the Moon

Our Nan

Your life has been traumatic in many ways
You've taken into your home everyone from waifs to strays
You brighten up our lives with all your kindness
You've been a dear kind mum to me
In ways perhaps not everyone can see
At first it was Gran Cavill you cared for
To the last- the list is endless
Aunt Ada, your own parents and your husband George
All cared for by you- you have such strength of mind
And now at eighty-four you're still the lynch pin
Of your family your love has reached
Out to embrace not only your children but now
Grandchildren and great grandchildren
Your life has touched so many people
May you still have many years to live
I'm sure you will – you are so sprightly still
All summed up in just a few words
Our mum and Nan forever

Sarah McBride

The Folk

The folk in there have brilliance
They shine as the stars above
Each cannot be as circumspect
Or discreet as they'd like to be
Whether well or ill each one of us
Has a redeeming quality – except when
The thrust of mental illness does not allow
Us to trust the rest of mankind
To our detriment and our own inward loss
It takes special people to look after us
When were in the torment and throes
Of these terrible terrifying voices
Our thoughts that come to enfold
Our very being – some say its like mental torture
It seems like that to me at times so
I'm grateful there's someone to care
The doctors and nurses are all stars
Though they may of this be aware
Were in this together one-to–one and so I propose
Please let us be friends – not foes

Trajectories to the Moon

Life's Legacy

The days go hurtling past apace
And I am still standing still
Days to months – months to years
And I am standing still
My life is a landslide
All is falling past me at a push
No waiting moments – moments take
Me with them at a rush
When and when will be the end?
I do not know for certain except
The certainty of death's dark instance
As is so for all of us
Days of my youth come back to haunt me
Happy, sad, unforgiving in their misunderstandings
A true saying, "youth is wasted on the young"
I am old, and will go back soon
From whence I sprung
Leaving only trust – trust I must
In something other
Than a legacy of dust

Sarah McBride

The Samaritans

They'll tell you they are always there
You can phone six times a day
Not an inkling given in this time
What they really think or say
You're a nuisance really at best
At worst a large imposter
But still they continue telling you
Were always here with sympathy
We understand so well
So do confide in us – were confidential
So lulled into security
You unburden your very heart
Only to find their sympathy
Doesn't run to that
If they don't like what you tell then
They disconnect the line
And limit you to just one call
And say that you'll be fine
It's for your greater good they'll say
For theirs for it's not ours
Don't trust in the Samaritans
It's all a total farce

Strange Thoughts

Strange thoughts, why, do you flit
So swiftly through my mind
Can't you sense the desolation
You always leave behind
Of greatness lost
A heartfelt nothingness
A confusion mighty
In its power to oppress
Somewhere, no doubt, within myself
The hidden fault lies deep
For thoughts you mill
To feed my quill
But you I cannot keep
For length of time to understand
The story I should say
It's my eager grasping such
That you should ever slide away
If striving to retain
I ever earn the right to pen
You my strange thoughts shall be word
But only then

Sarah McBride

Night time in Psychiatric unit

I must sleep tonight again
In this god forsaken place
Jehovah please rescue me
From the evil that is here
It is not immediately obvious
With the drapes so grandly sewn
That a caricature if all that's earth
Is here with its home
Hewn out as not with human hands out
A heart that's made of stone
Please bring them all to life again
As only you know how
Jehovah god, I beg you now
Have mercy – pity please now
As only you can know

Moustache Pending

Help! I'm growing a moustache
Did it develop suddenly or did
It surreptitiously arrive
Will it continue growing until it's bushy
So I can twirl it into handlebars
Is it my hormones which have gone awry
Or is it just some quirk of natures lie
To make me look more like a man
When all I ever want to be or am
Is just a woman

Jonathan – my son

Jonathan – your name means gift from god
And I see you as just that
There was just you and to begin with
Then daddy Brian appeared on the scene
And then you had a younger sister Angela
When Angela was still in the womb you left me
Cruelly struck down by meningitis and a coma
You were just eighteen months old
Just old enough for me to hope and dream for you
And to know your beautiful personality
You loved music – and the little song of the day was
Baby cant you see baby you and me
Have a groovy kind of love – you love music still
Even now I cannot write about the meningitis
Without tears stinging my eyes when I think
What might have been
You are thirty four years old now
With a mind of a two year old
Like Peter Pan – you will never grow up
But then you will remain forever innocent
You know no badness whatsoever
And you respond to my kindness – although you
Can make your displeasure known when someone is unkind
Your life has been one of terrible sadness
Maybe one day I will write in detail all you
Have been through in your young life
At the moment it is still to raw for my mind to process
Even after all these years I know I have not
Accepted it or grieved for you as the little boy you were
My love for you knows no bounds or barriers
You will be home my son to stay as soon as time allows
It is I now your dearest wish and also mine

Trajectories to the Moon

Heartfelt Protest

You took my little poems
That were so close to my heart
And made them into jigsaws
With many a missing part
Sometimes the tine too long to rhyme
I feel I must protest –
I didn't write it that way
With endings left unsaid
Perhaps it was my handwriting
It wasn't of the best
I'm looking for excuses
Fir the folk who did the rest
Perhaps I should have overseen
(A gaffer on the site)
But 'thank you' anyways toujours
You truly did your best I'm sure
But please don't show my little book
By all and sundry I'm forsook
I feel I must protest

Footsteps

Feet are members of the body
Indispensable to those
Whose feet are still intact
Many are maimed by the land mines
Princess Diana worked so tirelessly
To have destroyed
Her feet brought her kindly footsteps
To many far off lands
Following that dreadful
Accident in Paris
Her feet are no so sadly stilled
As with many "good" people
Whose footsteps last them
Just their lifetime
It is such a waste of a pair of feet
That just as experience has made
Their owners wiser – their footsteps are no longer heard
An irony that is often life

Trajectories to the Moon

The little pink chair

I was invited into the Psychiatrists lair
Where he indicated a little pink chair
There were three chairs there –
Unlike the three bears
Two were very comfy but the lowest one sank
In fact to floor level I just sank and sank
I was decidedly at a disadvantage at ones
As his loftier chair made the doctor seem twice
The man he had been when he asked me to sit
In the little pink chair – there was no avoiding it
Once does what ones told on occasions like this
It called institutionalisation to wit
I mist have looked a comical sight
In the little pink chair too low for my height
I know the doctor laughed at my plight
I suspect he was laughing well into the night
Or did he forget as I walked out the door
And think to himself "what a crashing bore!"

Din Dins

T'was sausages for dinner today
Like Churchill's cigar they did lay
Beside the mashed spud
(Are we chewing the cud)
Or ruminating about a great day

The pudding was something to die for
Jam Sponge recipe to decipher
We are what we eat
Eminent chefs have decreed
Whatever happened to Mrs Beeton

Trajectories to the Moon

Three Friends

Three friends sat upon a bench just talking
No embarrassing silence in between
Three friends who met in adverse situation
Each with a story all their own
Sharing thoughts and feelings with each other
Each with a story worthy to be told
I shall remember this evening
When the twilight glows – and I am once again
Out in the melee that is life
Why will I remember such an evening
I was one of those friends upon a bench

Sarah McBride

Dear Friend

I write to you from prison
Yes, I too have been in prison
What is euphemistically called
The prison where I am
Has within it a man
Reminiscent of you, dear son
My heart goes out to him
And having given him my love
As lent from you to him He will survive the coming
Tempest or endure the present one
To its finale
This man – for man he is
Though just a boy
Fights battles in his mind
Inspiring fear and awe
To all around
Fearsome and Awesome
Are his demons faced
With mighty arm each day
To face the foe and
Relive the Vietnam battle
He must go
So real to him
He has put names to those
Who would destroy his soul
The Vietcong
This boy who is a man
Has seen to much and
As he says has been to Hell
It is not a Hell of his own making
He is, he says, a prisoner of war
And so believes it is his right
To imprison any such unwary soul
By use of mundane, everyday affairs
Like cup of tea should it be black or white

Trajectories to the Moon

Pick that thing up its all part of the fight
Suffice, perhaps, for one day
This I write.

Sarah McBride

Touch of Time

Awareness of a wealth of wonder
In your eyes my dear
If I could only see with childlike truth
As now you do
This world might seem a better place
To live in dear
If you could lend me just a little
Thought or two
If you could lend me oh! Just simple
Share of thought from you
To see me through
Awareness of the touch of times sure
Toll on you my dear
If I could only lift the load of life
A little from your arms
This world might seem a safer
Place to live in dear
If I could warning ward off any
Sorrow sent to you
If I could warning ward off oh! Just
Simple share of hurt from you, this I would do
Awareness too, that thinking so
Is only dreaming dear I cannot live the life ahead for you
That's yours alone I too must bear the headache of
Your growing up my dear
Must watch and warn but let you
Work out your own way
Must watch and hope that you'll be
Justly proud of me some day
And I of you

Little Fishes

Trajectories to the Moon

Little fishes of the River
Swimming round the rocky scene
What you do is programmed in you
Instinct given by the power unseen
Every little fish and creature
Of the rivers dark recess
Has its place among the hierarchy
From the plankton to the rest.
Little fishes of the river
May you always pass the test
Of your life among the rushes
Always be there for we care
We'd miss you if you vanished
You enrich our lives and culture
Little fish beyond compare

Sarah McBride

Circus at Cushendall

It was red letter day
That came just once a year
When Fossett's circus came to Cushendall
Animals never before beheld
By any of us were there
The elephant I especially recall
For his little eyes they seemed
To laugh and glow
Was he remembering better times
When he roamed free
Or was he brought up in a zoo?
Now we the people
We were behind the bars
Whilst the elephant reigned supreme
It was his hour

Cold Little Feet

Cold little feet that had no shoes
Bundling by on their way to school
Through snow and ice it was the same
Feet that did not though
Being bare know any shame
Other pupils did now point at shoeless feet
Or ridicule in any way
We were, we thought, quite privileged
Our feet well clad with pity in our hearts
But nothing said horses were better shod
Than they – but then the horses feet were
Peoples means of livelihood they pulled the
Plough and clattered down the cobblestones
With cart attached taking folk from A to B
Those days have long gone from these islands
Now people have a variety of shoes
And odor eaters to insert in them
If perchance their feet perspired
"The Good Old Days" left much to be desired

Sarah McBride

Little Bird

Little bird so busy on the fence
Oblivious to any woe or strife
Though you're of another kind
You were made with us in mind
And you decorate the landscape that is life

As you fly first high then low
Take my thoughts enamored so
I can almost feel the freedom of your flight
Rest through the night until it's morn little one
Then sing for me your joyous song
At the chorus of the dawn

Trajectories to the Moon

People

People can impose poetry on others
Who are just not of poetic mind
This imposition it would be kinder not to do
I am of this ilk, and so must write
And choose those who can take the tear
Some are powerful as I write
And too telling for some others
I shall not impose on Doctors and Nurses again
Unless specifically asked

Sarah McBride

Childhood

Childhood should be a time of happiness
Something to hang the rest of your life upon
Childhood nowadays is filled with hyper-activity
Or just inactivity – couch potato being the
Phase used for this – how sad to see
The children of today – no scope for imagination, they
Computers – Pokemon and La-La fill their days
They do not have to think of games to play
Dressed as miniature adults from a few months old
So much expected of them they are not equipped to give
At heart they are the same as children of
A bygone age just beautiful and innocent
If we will let them be

Trajectories to the Moon

Attitudes

People with attitude are
Incomprehensible to me
I always hope for reasonable care
In what folk say about me here
My character has been blackened
Quite enough
At least I say
Enough is indeed enough
Whereas at one time I would
Have let things pass and rode
The storm of people's discontent I question now
And am as assertive as
My personality will allow
There are folk who hate it
If I seem well mentally
Able to take and make decisions
For myself
At last it seemed
To me that I was free
As free as I may ever be I can write –
I can say that now
I have a gift for poetry
I've been told
But some folk would love to see me fail
And have another mental downward trail
Especially people who are close to me
Or who think I am their property
To do with as they see fit
Even to the point that they'd commit
Me to the institute's grip
A little power corrupts a little
Absolute power corrupts absolutely
I have been a victim of other's power
For most of my life
Bending to everyone's will it seems to me

Sarah McBride

Enough is indeed enough –
I am wiser now
Than in youth – and so I am me
Take me as I am or not at all
Requiem doesn't seem that far-off after all.

Trajectories to the Moon

Alone

I could be very lonely here
But I am not so lonely here
As I have been in other places
Sometimes loneliness is to be preferred
To the company of some others
I have found friendship
Among the mentally ill
And some of those who care for us
(Although the nurses cannot let themselves be seen as friends)
I feel they are of friendly mind
At Astley House
And that will suffice
For this day as I write

Sarah McBride

Good Night - Sleep Tight

Half past three in the morning
And it feels as if I'm the only one abroad
I know this isn't true
So many people work all night
And folk in Mental Health Units can not sleep
It is part of the problem
And half past three in the morning
Is when we're at our lowest ebb
Morning comes as welcome respite
After the long, long night
Good night – sleep tight does not apply
At half past three in the morning

Trajectories to the Moon

Beginning

The T-wave was abnormal
On the graph of my heart
I do not despair
It was, as it were
Just waving to you
In acknowledgement
I had thought perhaps
"If you licked my heart
It would poison you"
(A phrase borrowed from
A holocaust survivor)
A pretentious melodramatic
Psychotic sentiment you say
Maybe so – how could I say or know
Except how it seems to me
If my heart still waves
(In psychiatric parlance "wobbly throw")
There is still hope for all of
Us in here
Whose hearts are bruised and broken
By those insensitive to others
We are not broken beyond repair
If our hearts still wave
Even, if only, on an E.C.G.

Sarah McBride

When Two Worlds Met

You are black and beautiful my friend Richard
And our friendship spans the years
We are both not perhaps as we were
Meant to be
Our minds meet on the cultural
Mine Irish – yours Indian and Nigerian
But we share a common heritage
Our mental illness
We understand each other on a level
Others do not comprehend
You with your battle with the voices
That come ever to plague you
Me with the intrusive thoughts
That are so pervasive
The staff nurse understands to an extent
And rescues you for a game of pool sometimes
You are a dear, dear friend
Even when I once again venture out
Into life's rain
As you eventually will too
I hope we shall remember the happy times
When we laughed together at the Rap
And Irish music
Two cultures merged together
Thank you for your company
May we ever remember these times
With affection
When our two paths met

Trajectories to the Moon

Fettered Foetus

Fettered foetus – before birth
Bonded to a woman's womb
Another creature fashioned soul to fetter serve
Birth bound to bear the cross
Of cultivation, class and spirit curb
Designation destiny of doing
Destination due to death deserve
Or so it seems who can say
Lie to die and so
Tongue tie eternity
As blinding bonds make black
Blithe spirits as with callous curtain
Through all this throng truth's torch
Shines sense of certain this that
That at the last some shed
Their fettering fronded fulcrum
That these same soar
Soul safe and sure
For first fast freedom

Sarah McBride

The Unread Rasp

Transient as flickering snow beside which black shines
Souls shiver, sore-saddled
Flesh geared to the galloping steer-clear of involvement
That's round-reckon of this decimal day!
That's hallmark of the computer age!
Clash and crash, strikes for fashionable claims are wars well won
Monetary amusements these of evolutions providence to
equip all, regardless of mens manner, with caprice.
To equate all with ample sustenance, and lust for a gain that must soon teem dust
The colour of the computer clay is rust, and spectral is today's programme.
Why fuss and fumble – grunt and grumble in harmony of
disagreement now when by tomorrow conscience – churn will
spoil-spurn all but that deemed edible. So pressing palatable
happenings on a future people as,
"The Good old Days" on us
Blast-off has taken over where the bugle-call let up but the
aggressive tone rasps on
So deafening is the roar of death in everything these days:
No one hears
The rasp of the rusty hinges as the door swings slowly to ajar
While the madness of it all sits, cosseted-secure
Within the unawakened silence of ourselves

Award

I saw an award in the Daily Mail
For a G.P. who was kindness itself without fail
To depressed people sometimes considered to be
Beyond the pale of society
My G.P. Dr Dawson
I thought of this ilk
In fact were he a Barrister he'd have taken silk
I wrote a commendation
I thought should win
Then committed an unforgiveable sin
I mentioned the company that dealt with the pills
And lo and behold!
They won with their skills
Or so Dr Dawson has ventured to say
And I can believe that – or not – as I may

Sarah McBride

Xmas in Ireland

Each year Santa came on the dot
And brought with him to many a cot
Apple, orange and toys
For the girl and the boys
Oblivious, we took what we got

Ah dream! At fifteen to be shattered
How we cried (as if it all mattered)
It wasn't dear Santa who left us our fanta
Or Aladdin who played in our Panto
T'was Dad all the time (he taught
me the rhyme)
Hiawatha I was somebody's daughter

Aaron (Support Worker) Brought in his guitar to Psychiatric Unit

Musing the musician sits
Nimble fingers waiting to interpret
As tunes race through his mind
Waiting to be sung in unison
With fingers plucking at the strings

The resultant music – sometimes down-to-earth
Sometimes profound
It really does wreak havoc or
Improve the mind
Depending on the hearer and the melody
We tap along or sing in harmony

Music has a power that is its own
It can raise the hearer's spirits
So they soar
Or wallow in the sentiments sublime
Of days gone by indeed the days or yore

Sarah McBride

The Dungeon

The smoke room draws us like a magnet
The cigarette smoke swirling round us all
It is the thing to do in here – it whiles the time away
Without it time would pass more slowly through the day
There's Maria, Mary, Chris and Wendy to mention but a few
We're all good friends as friendship matters here
We help each other sometimes more than nurses do
We each have similar experience and so
The smoke room far from being the dungeon some may see
Is a place of refuge where we all can go
And smoke a cigarette and tell our tales of woe
I know some think it quite a sin to smoke
But without it surely some would run amok
I love the folk I've met within this smoke room
They're just like bother and sister here to me

Arrogant? Nonsense

We are not born arrogant
It is an acquired trait
As children we do not patronize
Or arrogant be
Arrogance does not sit well
Upon a real man
So-called professionals
Sometimes suffer from
An arrogant attitude
To the detriment of those
They perhaps in all conscience
Seek to help
It is a terrible thing
To be so arrogant that
Everyone and everything must be
In subjection to your will
And absolute power over someone's life
May arrogance soon be a thing
Of the past
Along with the wickedness
That can be classed alongside it

Sarah McBride

Occupational Therapy

O.T. seems a futile activity
Tinsel and glue – to infinity
Where does it get you
It'll only upset you
If I tell you the message it brings
No-hopers are here for a rest
With everyone doing their best
O.T.'s a distraction (a great interaction)
Between all with exception of me

Trajectories to the Moon

More notes from Psychiatric Unit

Poised my pen sits above the paper
I have nothing specific in my mind
To write about I have had enough of psychological games
If they are such
So really I have reached a state of flux
Many are the thoughts that race across my mind
Searing it from memories so sad
They are not borne well upon remembrance
I wish to dance – I wish to sing
But decorum dictates this cannot be so
In the place where I am now
We are a motley crew and so do not always
Appreciate each others music or
Each others song
We all try to be friends with one another
But sometimes our different attributes intrude
And hurtful glance or word will then ensue
What is called 'hyper' is just super sensitivity
I am like that a phrase that's often used
In this fraternity – we understand
To an extent each other here
And when we don't?
When we don't a kindly word is asked for
And mostly given

Sarah McBride

Cobweb Cultivation

Drugs to make me sleep and some
To wake me up when I am sleeping
Drugs which make me eat and then
Behave ravenously at the tea table
Drugs to male me rant and rave
Drugs that make me not so brave
Drugs which can inhibit me
Not content with that
Drugs which can disinhibit me
Drugs that have made me sleep
Half of my waking life away
Drugs which cause no motivation
Drugs for cobweb cultivation
Drugs to fuddle my poor brain
So disclosure becomes no gain
Please help me leave them all behind
And help me write away the pain
In lighter vein

Dilemma

Should I go or should I stay
In this unit for the mentally ill
I am always wise with hindsight
And so I could regret the choice I make
At home I sit alone and listen to my music
Which is sad and haunting to the ear
Sometimes I wish I was back at the institution
That, I know is not a normal way of thinking
Here at least the others understand the 'thoughts'
Though for some they take the form of voices
The friends I've made all have many problems
Some long similar lines as my own
I think here I don't take enough 'time out'
From all the talking and so
I could become quite ill again
This afternoon the clouds seemed all but lifted
I felt more in control of all mu actions and my thoughts
This evening again the altered state of consciousness
Threatens to descend once more
I'm frightened and alone

Addiction

I'll just have one more
And then I will stop
It's the lat one for me
My intention is
But these cigarettes
Have a mind of their own
Even dog ends look good
To me now I'm on hold
Nicotine – nicotine – you've ruled
Long enough – my life's not
My own while I crave for a puff
Today, I must stop with some
Helpful advice
A non-smoker I'll be
Yippee I'll be free

Trajectories to the Moon

Untitled

It is with trepidation that I face tomorrow Thursday
It could make or break me in the weeks and years to come
I know the doctors and the nurses will do the very best they can
To transfer my care to where I feel much more at home
The tenor of the wand is different here at Boston
From what I had become accustomed to
To my mind the people here are kinder, gentler, so
Of course I feel this is a better place to be when I am ill
This illness which has so many facets
Has dogged me now for thirty years and so
I see no end to it this side of the grave
I can only hope for some good times in between each episode
And hope you'll care for me and love me with
Agape love as much as it is in your power to do
I know that what I write sometimes may seem I'm
Judging harshly the very ones who are at the forefront
Of my care. At the time its how it seems to me
It's a real to me and so I hope you will accept
My apologies if indeed you feel I haven't always
misunderstood
The way things have to be in this fraternity

Miniature Adults

Childhood should be a time of happiness
Something to hang the rest of your life upon
Childhood nowadays is filled with hyper-activity
Or just inactivity – couch potato being the
Phrase used for this – how sad to see
The children of today – no scope for imagination, they
Computers – Pokemon and La-La fill their days
They do not have to think of games to play
Dressed as miniature adults from a few months old
So much expected of them they are not equipped to give
At heart they are the same as children of
A bygone age just beautiful and innocent
If we will let them be

Trajectories to the Moon

We're the Samaritans

We're the Samaritans do tell
We listen to your bell
We do it rather well – do tell
Are you suicidal, come do tell?
You're not – not yet, oh well!
We'll remedy that at once do tell
Only potential suicides are welcome here – don't tell
Not feeling suicidal yet? Ah hell!

Dr. Dawson

I saw an award in the Daily Main
For a G.P. who was kindness itself without fail
To depressed people sometimes considered to be
Beyond the pale of society
My G.P. Dr. Dawson I thought of this ilk
In fact were he a barrister he'd have taken silk
I wrote a commendation I thought should win
Then committed an unforgivable sin
I mentioned the company that dealt with the pills
And lo and behold! They won with their skills
Or so Dr. Dawson has ventured to say
And I can believe that – or not-as I may

Trajectories to the Moon

Why No Empathy ?

Why do they not pre-empt the situations
There was no need for the patient
To go out into the cold
They (the nurses) could have talked to her
And made her feel so much more at home
Is it a power trip for them
Or is there something I don't know
Why? Why? Is what I ask myself
Can't they put themselves in other people's shoes
They are supposed to have a training
Is this the way the training makes them act
I know I speak from only the patient's perspective
But I think also from a human aspect too
Is it abuse of the power the job has brought them?
I do not wish to think this so
I see people as people be they nurse or client
Until the 'tem' and 'us' is gone for good
No-one will really be safe in institutions

Colour of Kindness

What colour is kindness
It comes in all shades
Except perhaps the bleak black
Pf darkness – which is ignorance
To be truly ignorant of the
Colour of kindness
Us a great affliction
Brought on by some experiences
In childhood or teenage years
When one is vulnerable and innocent
Those who rob the innocence of childhood
Or the teenage years are reprehensible
But maybe not to the extent
It always seems
They too, perhaps, were not shown
The true colour of kindness
In their lives and so perpetuate
The dreadful cycle of abuse
Devoid of empathy or loving – kindness
They lurch through life
From one catastrophic circumstance
To yet another one
They seek solace in relationships
They are not adequately equipped to form
Leaving behind a trail of devastation
The end result of which is mental breakdown
Being shown the true colour of kindness
At such a time can transform a life
Sadly this is rarely been
In the system of things new and existing
May things change soon for better times
Before one in three becomes everyone whilst the madness of it all
Sits, cosseted, secure
Amidst the unawakened silence of ourselves

Trajectories to the Moon

I didn't mean to cause offence

I didn't mean to cause offence
But then I never o
Yet many folk take umbrage
At things I say though true
At least It's how it seems to me
I never can get through a day
Without ill feeling holding sway
Quite innocent remarks can cause commotion
As to why its so u haven't got a notion
My friends I can count on just five fingers
Five days I haven't smoked but enmity still lingers
There's no escape for me from this living hell
There is no one I can safely tell
Jehovah if you are there for me
Make then know – make them see
How damaged I am by neuroleptics and how
The system has forgotten me.

Autumn

If you've never seen "the Fall" in Massachusetts
You haven't seen a fall at all I say
Our Autumn here in England is colourful
But we don't have the vivid reds and yellows in the leaf
A blaze with colour takes on a new dimension
I never thought to see such spectacle
But then I saw a different kind of fall
Niagara Falls – now there's an even greater spectacle
In the little boat 'Maid of the Mist' we went
Right up in to the falls – the roar of the falls
And the absolute power of it
I fee privileged to have seen both spectacles
Memories are precious and will last forever

2 Bad

It's as of nowadays everyone has to be
Genetically modified
Eight legs now where
Once two would suffice
It seems like that to me
Two legs do the work of eight
You're either on your feet all day
Or sitting at a fax machine
Churning out messages on
Your mobile phone
You don't have to get the spelling right
Its abbreviated nonsense that's in sight
Addling the minds of old and young alike
Where will it all lead
When all computers crash and there is nothing left
People having lost the art of conversation
Everyone will reap the dark consequences
If this inevitable technology night

Acorn

Ive come here this morning to 'Acorn'
A day care centre for the mentally ill
Although they have welcomed me here
And Indeed I have nothing to fear
I do feel somewhat isolated
In a little cocoon of my own
I am hoping for metamorphosis
To become once again the butterfly I used to be
I think it's too late – too many breakdowns
To much adversity – I do not fit in anywhere
Least of all here – but ive thought like this before
And before long I knew all the names of new friends
Let's hope it will turn out like that here too.

In smoke room of Psychiatric Unit

Words do not come easily
In social activity here
Stilted conversation
Us our stick in craw each day
People seem not to be
As they should or ought to be
Articulation and humour
Not our forte here

Reactions

My temper flared so easily
It is totally alien to me
It was over such a petty thing
People in here are so volatile myself included
Nurses should not treat them as they do
I had been standing at the trolley
And I was totally ignored for someone else
That would not adversely affect me as a rule
I think perhaps the medication is affecting me
And making me aggressive too
I would not adversely affect me as a rule
I think perhaps the medication is affecting me
And making me aggressive too
I would not hurt anyone especially not Maria
But who would believe that in here
There is no ne who seems to understand
Why, why, will no one listen to us and change
Their attitude – it would make life so much
Easier for all of us – nurses included

Lone Magpie

I never want to see a lone magpie
In the hollow
It is, I'm told a harbinger of doom
Two-yes-that's thought to be a good omen
But one spells an absolute disaster
I should not have had those implants
To make me more voluptuous
Is spied a lone magpie on my way
To see the doctors
Me silicones have leaked
And ah'm in trouble
That magpie has a lot to answer for
Why couldn't it have had a double.

Sarah McBride

For a special night nurse

Angie- tall and willowy,
Dressed from head to toe in black
(Ready for the night shift)
How kind you were when you sat
With us – the patients
Last Friday night
We could not know it would be
A time seared on our memory,
A night we would never forget
We cannot but see the parallel
With our own lives as we live on
(But you are as only sleeping)
Angie – we all love you – still do
And surely will again!

Trajectories to the Moon

My Personality

I know my personality is flawed now
After all the E.C.T. I've had
Also the neuroleptics I must take
To keep the psychosis at bay
It's really not my fault
Although some think I'm here by default
Some people can be so hurtful
I am slung into writing as I do
I really do not wish to hurt anyone
Verbally or the written word
I really don't – in a little song
The lyric says – nothing seems to
Go right for me for long
With mental illness even the best of friends
Sooner or later get a sufficiency of us
It is never my intention to alienate my friends
Yet this is what I seem to do
The little censor seems to have gone
That part of my brain which can oversee
What is said and written by me
I did not mean to cause offence
Hence the "jumped up nothing"
Which is me in northern Irish parlance
The Ulsterman who wouldn't
Want to have me under his oxter
Who knows what life will bring to him
Tho I wish him well
And would not harm him
In anyway whatsoever

Sarah McBride

Rewrite my life

Rewrite my life why don't you?
Ill never write yours that's for sure
Why not have a go at that
Mouth of yours –
Zips and buttons are easily found
Don't be put off by the size of it
Belt up – or just quietly drown
In your lying words
A stream of abuse you propound

Trajectories to the Moon

Lies to the face

Stick your nose up in the sir
Careful – it's so sharp
You just may puncture the skit
Are you responsible for
The downpours recently
Or maybe – just maybe – much more
Look down your nose at me
Focus your gaze on your breast
Then beat it in time to some music
A lament for causing distress
You disturbed my peace
With your letters
Now in this little address
I'm endeavouring to redress the balance
You really are quite unblessed
I'll end this poem – wishing you well
Though it's not what you wish to me
Ah yes! Gossip about me
Lies to the face – something I've had to endure

Sarah McBride

Belvoir Castle

Belvoir Castle up on the hill
Steeply the path rose to meet us
Round a corner and there it was
The castle in all its glory
The admission fee was affordable
And for the spectacles we saw
Was quite laudable
Crimean, Boer wars till the
Present day were represented
By the uniforms and crusades
It gave us a glimpse into history
Henry the Eighth looked down
From the wall his portrait
So realistic - it was as if
He could step out of the picture
Propose marriage – then chop off my head

Trajectories to the Moon

Tribute to Lincs line

When I think of the help lines I have phoned
None can compare to Lincs Line for renown
The men and women who answer all the calls
Are kind and treat us gently as we recall
The adversity and hurt which have led us to this pass
I wish I could do justice to them with my little poem task
Words cannot convey my appreciation for these people
There's Joe and Rose – Denise, Pat and Keith
Karen and Barbara – all come to mind – they are so kind
To me Lincs line has been a hiding place from the storm of life
Long may they continue to do the life saving work they do
Thank you each and everyone at Lincs line just for being you.

Sarah McBride

A Beautiful day (stolen)

A beautiful day was stolen from him
By an older man who was sad and bad
How you may ask does he remember
Such a painful memory?
In summer shorts and t-shirt
When he reaped his harvest an innocent
The sky was blue the sun shone bright
On that July day he was as happy as could be
This man who thought he's like
The things he did to him
He has forgiven long ago
But just cannot forget
How it affected him
He stood outside himself
As if this were happening to someone else
An ability he retains to this day
He feels he is stuck emotionally
At just nine years

The sun went out for that little boy that day
And never has returned.

Trajectories to the Moon

Good Bye My Friend Seroxat

I am coming off Seroxat
The withdrawal symptoms show
Thanks to Panorama's skill
The majority now know
When some try to reduce this pill
Oblivion they will seek
Many will know that is true
This exit of which I speak
I have been taking seroxat
Best part of a year or more
Must say, in a way, it's been helpful
Changed my personality core
From being monosyllabic and shy
I'm verbose as never before
Alienating most of my friends
With rhyming couplets galore
I'm really on my soapbox now
Though I'm writing at a table
Ill tell you now how to conduct your lives
And counsel with labels
Never mind of no qualifications only living life thus far
I'm thinking of renaming myself
Sigmund Freud or some such other
Though my qualifications are in short supply
This does not me deter
By virtue of my taking it
Seroxat makes me dare
Beware for I'm so knowledgeable now
As I swipe my troubled brow
I'll soon out do that lot of you
I'm a talking dictionary now

Sarah McBride

Jonathan and my illness

You liked my poem
"Two little shoes" are missing
I wrote it out of the depths
Of the sorrow – for my son
Who had a mind of
A two year old
Having had meningitis at
The early age of eighteen months
Sometimes I allow myself to speculate
On how things might have been
Jonathan loves music and I think
Somehow that would have been
His interest in life
Maybe he would have played
Various musical instruments
As my brothers – his uncles do
He certainly has a sense of humour
He laughs (heartily) at incongruity
As I do myself
I have a mental illness
Which makes the situation doubly difficult
I have tried my best not to
Abandon him – mu mamma
Used to say – before all words
I taught him were forgotten
I love my little son – although
Physically he is a man
He will forever remain a child
I have found telephone friends
At Sane line who seem to understand
The dilemma I have – especially
How Bi-polar Affective Disorder
Can take over my mind sometimes

Trajectories to the Moon

Flynn and Fly

Two beautiful dogs -
Flynn and Fly
Brothers who did everything together
Brothers who are no longer united Fly has died in a most
Ignominious way
Killed by an oncoming speeding
Car – in the beautiful
Countryside where he was on holiday
Flynn – Margaret and Dick
Were suddenly bereft and left to grieve
Life will never be quite the same
For his special people
Who loved him as a precious
Special dog indeed Flynn keeps on looking for
His brother Fly in all
His usual hiding places
Expecting him to reappear at
Any moment
His companion has gone and Flynn cannot understand why
It is heartbreaking to see
The image of his brother Flynn has almost identical
Markings to Fly
Both were inseparable pets in life
Though now Fly will no longer
Walk the streets of Heckington
With Margaret
He was a much loved dog
In life in death he will be remembered
Every time his little elegy is read
And Fly no.2. Will walk
With Flynn
Happily in Heckington

Footsteps

Feet are members of the body
Indispensable to those
Whose feet are still intact
Many are maimed by the landmines
Princess Diana worked tirelessly
To have destroyed
Her feet brought her kindly footsteps
To many far off lands
Following that dreadful
Accident in Paris
Her feet are now so sadly stilled
As with many "good" people
Whose footsteps last them
Just their lifetime
It is such a waste of a pair of feet
That just as experience has made
Their owners wider – their footsteps
Are no longer heard
An irony that is often seen in life

Trajectories to the Moon

Feathered Armour

My housework is laborious in the extreme
My armour feather duster, bleach and scouring crème
Usually such armour stays where put upon a shelf
Until a burst of energy occurs within myself
Then round I go as someone quite possessed
The carpet, surfaces and kitchen floor all blessed
Not a self-respecting speck of dust my cloth defies
My duster mop and bucket then disguise
My lack of motivation for this mundane task
Was I put upon this earth to be skivvy I then ask
The Answer is its necessary work for all to do
Or so it seems – everyone else's house is so pristine
I think it's shame that puts me to the test
Still I think I'll do it all again tomorrow
Or next week or year – when I have had a timely rest

Sarah McBride

Families

Were family people sat as if that excuses everything.
A good family is a blessing and can be relied upon
In the majority of cases though not all
"There exists a friend who is sticking closer
Than a brother" to quote from the holy book
I am very privileged to belong to a
Large family – there are eleven of us
Trouble is we are scattered to the four
Corners of the universe
There is a completely different type of family
The family of drugs – are they called
'Family' because it makes them seem innocuous!
Where would we the mentally ill people be
If we did not have the drugs to see us through
But please don't call them family-
Things take on a new dimension
When the word family is mentioned

Trajectories to the Moon

Transient Dream (Or Whispers of Despair)

Two heads bent together
Over childhood joy's
Two little faces without a trace
Of tearful toil
Intent on making castles
To be toppled at a stroke
Intent on living moments here and now

Two loves interwoven
Thro' few childhood years
Two young playmates captured
For a future reverie
Content to shell the sand
And see their boat list crazily
Speak Whispers! Speak Despair!
But don't dispel their transient dream

Sarah McBride

Social Workers

I had an advocate in you
Sister Angela Jonathan
Then two social workers decided
You were legally my next of kin
And it would take a court
To decide otherwise
I had visions of you being
Dragged before some tribunal
And being assessed as incapable
Of being my next – of – kin
Evil – pure evil is what they are
To even think they'd put you
Through an ordeal like that
Hate is something that corrodes
And eats away at trust
I try not to hate – but now
And again I cannot trust
Because of how you and I Jonathan
Have been treated in the past
By the very professionals
Who are supposed to have
Our interests at heart
I would lie down and die
For you Jonathan
If that would help but it is
Not an option
While I have breath left
In my body I will fight for you
As I have done all your life
I love you Jonathan, what do they
Know of love?!!
As Dickens said in his "Martin Chuzzlewit"
With affection beaming out of one eye
And calculation looking out of the other
That sums up Social Workers

Trajectories to the Moon

Garden of my thoughts

Stone, Stone – Rock of my childhood
You sat stoical – in the garden of my youth
You were polished white by the elements
And those who sat on you as you doubled
As a summer seat
You featured as anything we wanted you to be
Straddle you and you became a horse
Spread a tablecloth over you
And you became a table
You had so many uses – you were
Part of our lives
I went back to that garden
Looking for you a few years ago
You must have been removed –
You were no longer there
One might think how can anyone
Wax lyrical about a stone
You were more than just a stone to me
And I imbued you with qualities
That perhaps you did not have
I loved you as one of the
Familiar things of my childhood
I have never seen another rock like you
(The Plymouth rock in Boston Mass
Perhaps has a similarity though
Of another hue)
Maybe you grace some other garden now
In any case you grace
The garden of my thoughts

Sarah McBride

Benji Boy

I remember when I first saw you Benji
As a little scrap of a thing
In the crook of my son Tim's arms
To be honest I didn't quite know what to do with you
Never having had a puppy before
I treated you as if you were a new addition to the family
Just as I would a child
You are ten now and have given us
So much love and companionship
So much so – I cannot imagine life without you
You are a kindly dog and you seem
Almost to sense when something is going
To happen to anyone of us
You watch from the window until all of us
Are safe indoors at night
And enjoy your walks and your bones
And especially best ham from the fridge
Which I give you as a special treat sometimes
You are still boisterous as the little puppy you were
May you still have many years left
In which we may enjoy your company
You came to us all those years ago out of the blue
When its time for you to go
May you go peacefully, painlessly
A fitting end for the kindly gentle dog you are

Even the Music

Even the music is tainted
So you cannot taste its tune
And supper looks like Blitzkrieg
A salmon sandwich fugue
I do not wish to mention any names
They may not wish me well
Hades will give up its dead
But here they are in hell
Please give me strength to tell them
Of a brighter hope so sure
Better days to come within
A short sharp span of years
Please bring Armageddon
Even some who are here go down
To perish as to justice done
And your power and might be shown

Sarah McBride

Traffic Lights

Lights, lights and more lights
If you stop for one red
Chances are the next six lights are red
Same appertains to green lights
Pass one and you'll have a clean run through
Necessary things these lights
But do we have to have so many
Spaced between such small intervals of time
I'm not a driver myself and so perhaps
There are lots of points of view that would disagree
To plead ignorance would not stand up in court
If prosecuted for driving through red lights
As some people are won't to do
Through impatience or lack of responsibility
If stopped by a policeman they are quite irate
And do it all again as soon as they are free
Red, amber, green – the colours chosen
For this scheme are striking and so
There's no excuse for driving as if you
Are the only person on the road.

Trajectories to the Moon

Billet Doux

I shall miss you
When you are no longer here
And look for you
And hope to see your face
I shall see you in
The chair where in you sat
When you were here
And the dress you wore
Tell me you will be back soon
And so I will wait
Laughing for the afternoon
In the event that you do not show
I shall be bereft
More than perhaps you know
I will look for you
But will not find
For you will have gone
To where I do not know
But here you are
I here your sprightly step
Upon the path
And my heart skips a beat
And it dawns on me
I love you.

Sarah McBride

Colour of creation

All creatures of the earth
United in the bond of life
No evolutions theories to contend with
Your instinct given by a power above
Unseen, it's true, but surely
His sense of humour is beyond compare
Beauty, too, is seen in the creation
Have you ever seen the fall
In Massachusetts – the colours
Of the leaves – red, brown and gold
Such splendour provided for us to behold
Jehovah could have made everything
In black and white
Colour is a gift – we should enjoy
That aspect of our sight it's truly full of wonder
And now – just a look over yonder
At ducks waddling along from side to side
Peacocks spreading their tail feathers into fans
All make us rich – we do not have to pay
To see these sights
All are the free gift from our creator Jehovah God
How magnificent your
Creation really is
You know when even a little sparrow falls
You care for them just as you do for us
It is wicked men who kill and plunder
You will thunder at them
Then paradise forever
Will be – thine and mine

Dusty

Dear Dusty – you belong to Steve
And he takes the greatest care of you
You are lent to use at weekends
When your timely visit is a welcome
Sight for all of us
You are a kind and gentle dog
And you enjoy the things dogs do
Like walks and share of whatever
Foods are good for you
You add a luster to life
For Steve and for all of us
In our sojourn here
You are older now Dusty like myself
But indeed we hope you have
Some years in which we may
Enjoy your company
Long may you continue to visit us
It is a pleasure to have met you
I will never forget you

Sarah McBride

Broken Promises

We wouldn't ask for time if we didn't need it
Somewhere in the hurry – scurry of the ward
The truth of this is lost
People do not realise how they can make or break us
By broken promises and dialogue left unsaid
Patients com and go and also nurses
The tenor of the world can change from shift to shift
Why, why do they not know it is not kindness
To say they'll see us and then leave without
So mush as a goodbye for now and see you later
A common courtesy would have thought – and also others
Raking away a wooden barrier at the nurses station
Is a clever ploy to try to make us even
Until attitude changes 'them' and 'us' will always be alive
We are the enemy it seems to me and so we see
Not all – but some – of some of the nurses as the enemy too
Just let them spend a week as a patient on this ward
It should be part of all their training and also
Would maybe let them see things from the patients
perspective
I could rant and rave but I choose not to
Perhaps I will just sing and dance instead

Breakfast in Cushendall

Breakfast – the first meal of the day
Should be seen as sacred to us all
It stokes the fires of our energy
Setting a scene for stamina & recall
Our memories wouldn't be so burnished bright
If breakfast we did not partake of well
My mother always said breakfast before school
Would make us better scholars and so
The porridge – bacon – eggs were on her menu
Bright and sacrosanct our breakfast in Cushendall

Sarah McBride

A Beautiful Day

A beautiful day
Was stolen from her
By a man in a horse and cart
So many years ago

How you may ask
Does she remember such
A painful memory

She was a little girl
In floral frock
And sandals red
When he reaped his harvest
On an innocent

The sky was blue
The sun shone bright
On that august afternoon
She was happy as could be

This man who thought she'd like
The things he did to her
She has forgiven long ago
But just cannot forget
How it affected her

She stood outside herself
For the first time in her young life
As if this were happening
To someone else
An ability she retains to this day

She was a 'promising' pupil
She was told
Until that dreadful day

Trajectories to the Moon

She could not learn anything new
When she returned to school

She is stuck at that time
Emotional maturity not matching
Intellectual capacity
She fears she has not advanced
Beyond eleven years

The sun went out that August day for me
And never returned

Sarah McBride

Untitled

Jagged rocks and birds in flight
And water all around the windswept scene
Looks cold and uninviting
So I wouldn't like to step
Inside the picture – looks as if
A storm is brewing –
Thunder and lighting imminent
I'd like to see the same scene
In Spring or Summer of the year
A rainbow of peace is in the background
Which redeems itself bright and bold
And the birds are surely looking for
That elusive crock of gold.

www.ingramcontent.com/pod-product-compliance
Lightning Source LLC
Chambersburg PA
CBHW020442220526
45464CB00002B/814